Are You a Spiritual Entrepreneur?

Six Shifts to a Six-Figure Spiritual Business

Kimberly Maska

Published and distributed in the United States by Spiritual Biz Publishing, Inc.

ISBN 978-1-950756-06-3 (IngramSpark) PAPERBACK
ISBN 978-1-950756-01-8 (IngramSpark) HARDCOVER
ISBN 978-1-950756-02-5 (Smashwords)
ISBN 978-1-950756-03-2 (Amazon Print)

Library of Congress Cataloging-in-Publication Data

Names: Kimberly Maska, author.

Title: Are You a Spiritual Entrepreneur?: The Six Shifts to a Six-Figure Spiritual Business / Kimberly Maska.

Description: 1st Edition. | Asheville, North Carolina: Spiritual Biz Publishing, Inc., 2019

PUBLISHING

The publisher for authors dedicated to shifting consciousness.

For more of our products visit spiritualbizpublishing.com

I dedicate this work to my creative, spiritual, and life partner, Daniel. Thank you for believing in me and inspiring me every step of the way.

Contents

Introduction

"The biggest adventure you can ever take
is to live the life of your dreams."

— OPRAH WINFREY

IF YOU PICKED up this book, you probably consider yourself a spiritual person. You might also consider yourself an entrepreneur. Or at least you would *like* to be an entrepreneur in the near future. But do you consider yourself a *spiritual entrepreneur?* Do you know what a spiritual entrepreneur actually is?

If someone owns a doughnut shop, but also meditates, couldn't that person consider themself a spiritual entrepreneur? Well, sure, I suppose so. But that's not what we're talking about here.

What we *are* here to discuss, first and foremost, is the mindset that creates a successful spiritual entrepreneur. This will look different for everyone. But there is one important thing all spiritual entrepreneurs have in common: They are making a positive impact in the world and raising the global vibration through not only their lives, but also their careers.

There are mental, emotional, physical, and spiritual changes that need to be made to build and grow a thriving business. Especially a thriving business that is aligned with Source. This book is going to touch on all of it.

What a lot of people don't realize is there are some major shifts that need to take place before most people can allow financial abundance into their lives. Because of this, we're going to cover the *six shifts* my spiritual coaching clients are using today to build their six-figure spiritual businesses. Having amazing spiritual businesses allows them to help shift consciousness on this planet and raise its vibration. That's what we're here on Earth to do, right? It is our duty, as awakened individuals, to expand consciousness and have a global impact.

Now, I want to make something clear. This book might bring up some ideas that don't always fit together in your mind—specifically money, spirituality, and success. What can I say? It's a contentious topic, I know.

This subject matter may ruffle your feathers a little, but I promise I'm going to help shift your perspective. By the time you are done reading this book, you're going to see why having a successful spiritual business is absolutely *necessary* to help with the vibrational shift of this planet.

Before we move on, let's make sure you're in the right place. I want you to know who this material is for *before* we get going any further.

Who This Book is For

Well, let's get down to the big question: Are you a spiritual entrepreneur? At the beginning, I touched on the definition of a spiritual entrepreneur somewhat. But I'm going to get a little more in-depth now. There are some particular attributes a high-earning spiritual entrepreneur needs to have:

1. They know it's their mission to raise global awareness. They know they have a gift—a gift to share with others.

2. They also know Source blessed them with this gift for a reason. That is why it is their duty to share it with the world.

3. Finally, they understand that everything in the Universe needs to be in balance. Everything.

The Law of Compensation is always in play, and that means there must be an energy exchange between two parties. When you give, you must receive. That includes your spiritual gifts. I will go much more in-depth on this part later.

Do these attributes resonate with you? If so, then keep reading. If not, keep reading anyway. You will probably fall into these categories by the time you're done with this book.

This is for you if you are a healer, spiritual teacher, or coach who is done playing small, and you're ready to shift consciousness around the world by creating a movement with your message. You are ready to step it up in a *big* way.

I mean *movement*, as in really stepping out there—being the next Colette Baron-Reid, the next Sonia Choquette, the next Esther Hicks. *I mean really getting ready to step up to the plate and create a ripple effect on the planet, because that's why we're here.*

That means no more dabbling in your spiritual business because, really, no one ever created anything great by dabbling.

Do you know any famous dabblers? No? Neither do I.

It's finally time to master your business so you can

go from serving a few to serving thousands. All the while creating the financial abundance you deserve.

If you are struggling to attract consistent clients and create continuous financial abundance—which are the two primary things I hear across the board from spiritual entrepreneurs—and you have a spiritual business, then I want you to pay close attention. This book may change your life.

So what *are* we going to talk about here? By all means, let me explain.

We are going to cover:

- How to transform your spiritual coaching business and take it from an expensive hobby (which I know a lot of you have, right? You have been dabbling, so what you have is a very expensive hobby.) and shift it into an $8,000–$10,000-and-more-a-month business while serving your clients at a higher level.

- Why earning less than six figures is being selfish. Yes, I said *selfish*. We're going to go over more of that in a minute, but it's true. I promise when you hear it, you will have a life-changing aha moment.

- The real reason why you're struggling to manifest financial abundance, and what you can do to turn it around *today*.

- The *one thing* you really need to serve people around the globe. This is not more certifications. I know so many of you out there have a ton of certifications, but I bet you're missing this one thing. And this is why your business is stuck where it is and why you are not finding clients.

- How to create total freedom in your spiritual coaching business. Work less while receiving more financial abundance so you can give the energy of money back into the world. We are not here to be slaves to our businesses. It's supposed to be fun and allow you to be the best version of you.

- How to do all this while staying 100 percent true to your spiritual calling and serving your clients at a much higher level than you are now. I know that's a considerable concern for spiritual entrepreneurs. They feel like they're selling out. Somehow, we have been conditioned to think that creating and marketing a business, especially a spiritual business, goes against our spiritual calling. But that is a *myth!* You absolutely *can* do all of this while maintaining alignment with your soul-purpose.

In these pages, I'm going to show you how you *can* hold true to your spiritual calling and invite financial abundance into your life at the same time.

My promise to you, while we're together here, is a step-by-step plan for your $100,000 spiritual coaching business. But before we get going, let's set an intention together.

You hold the keys to the Universe at all times.

This is so important. We are coming together and sharing energy, space, and time. So take a moment and set that intention now. Just close your eyes, take a deep breath, and connect with your higher self. Set a positive intention that you will actively receive life-changing benefits from reading this book—and you will!

Remember, you hold the keys to the Universe at all times, so use them!

Finally, to be certain you get the absolute most out of this information, there are a few more things

I want to cover. I ask you to be open to receiving new information. Come with your cup empty. Put your self-limiting beliefs behind you. It could have a significant impact on you.

Also, be open to talking about success, money, and spirituality in the same breath, because I know that's a tough combination to view together. Sometimes it feels like it's an oxymoron—like something doesn't add up—but please, be open to it. I promise I'm going to help shift your perspective around all these concepts.

The people I will tell you about in this book are extraordinary spiritual entrepreneurs. They are some impressive individuals; they worked hard, they really care, and they earned their results. I shared some beautiful time with them during their journeys. They inspire me every day, and they have filled my life and career with meaning. The best part is, these students of mine are now having the same kind of energy exchange with their own clients. And I want the same for you.

So when you see the results, just know that we're all 100 percent responsible for ourselves, and that means that you're 100 percent accountable for your results, too. This is a reality check. If you aren't where you want to be in your spiritual business, then you have to look within and come to understand why you aren't there yet. It is time for you to shift. And you are in the right place to accomplish this. Now it's our turn to share some time together, so thank you for taking a moment to give yourself this gift. Let's take a deep breath and move right in.

Why This Book *is* for You

Does this sound like you? You feel like you're working harder than ever at your spiritual business, but you just don't have the income or the clients to show for it?

Have you been relying on the Law of Attraction to find clients because marketing feels a little icky, and you don't know how to do it in a way that feels good to you?

Are you afraid to charge what your coaching sessions are worth because you think you aren't supposed to charge for your spiritual gifts? Or maybe you don't even believe your gift is worthy of an energy exchange?

Do you think if you raise your prices, your clients will disappear? That's a widespread fear I hear all the time.

Do you ever doubt your abilities because sometimes you can't manifest the clients and income you want when you need it most? Heck, that might even be what you're teaching—manifesting abundance—and yet, you're struggling with it?

And, finally, do you know you could serve the world (and yourself) at a much higher level, but you're just not sure what the next step is?

Perhaps you are beginning to wonder if spiritual coaching as a profitable business just isn't possible.

Do you sometimes have trouble explaining the real impact of what you do? Or feel like people don't really get it? Maybe they don't really understand you? Perhaps they are even afraid of or creeped out by your gifts?

Perhaps you are beginning to wonder if spiritual coaching as a profitable business just isn't possible.

Well, I want to tell you, *none of those things are the real problem.*

The real problem is that you haven't made the right shifts. Once you make these shifts, you will have a proven process to create passive income in your spiritual coaching business, and you will attract high-paying, ideal clients who value what you do. Not only will they value you, but they will also get fantastic results because you're serving them at the highest level.

You will realize that the only thing holding you back is *you*. This is the hardest one to take in, isn't it?

As the creator of your reality, you have the power, knowledge, and strategies to make your six-figure spiritual coaching business a part of your physical reality today. It is just a matter of remembering to keep in alignment with Source and believe in yourself. It really is that easy . . . once you make the necessary shifts.

Don't believe me yet? That's okay. I believe in you.

You picked up this book because Source drew you here. It was absolutely no accident. We are all drawn to the tools and teachers we need, if we can learn to *pay attention to the signs*.

Your gifts were given to you by Source for a reason. And just like your stumbling upon this book was no coincidence, your spiritual abilities and understanding aren't random, either. But the kicker is, the Law of Compensation is always at play. There has to be an appropriate and balanced energy exchange. And I can tell you right now, there isn't if you are giving your gift away for free.

Here's an example I like to give: Think about the difference between a pair of shoes you may have bought at JCPenney versus a pair of Manolo Blahnik shoes. You would probably spend around $30 for the JCPenny shoes, am I right? But the pair of Manolo Blahniks, well, I don't think they have a pair of shoes for under $600.

When you wear the JCPenney shoes, you don't think much about taking care of them when you walk around. You might step in a puddle, get them dirty, accidentally kick something. When they get scuffed, you just throw them in the back of your closet on the floor. But who cares?

However, when you're wearing those Manolo Blahniks, you are hyper-aware of your surroundings at all times. You watch where you step, you avoid dirt and puddles, and then, when you get home, you put them on a shelf somewhere or perhaps even back in their shiny white box.

My point is, you invested a lot more money in the second pair, so you take a lot better care of them, right? You value the Manolo Blahniks so much more. And that's my point. Value. We as humans value what we invest the most in.

How many online courses out there have you signed up for? How many free online downloads or ebooks have you downloaded just from giving your email address on a website? You probably don't even know. The courses you only spent $20 on are probably still waiting for you to log in. All those free ebooks? Have you even read a single one? Didn't think so. Me either.

But if you invest a few months' rent or more into something, I bet you are sure as heck going to do your best to get the most out of it!

Now think about this in relation to your spiritual gifts. If you're out there giving your gifts away for free, or charging very little, how valuable does that make your gift look to others? You don't want to be a dog-and-pony show.

Wait, what?

That's right. A dog-and-pony show.

Someone I worked with a while ago said to me her biggest aha moment was when a friend of hers asked her to do tarot card readings at his daughter's birthday party. She agreed to it because she wanted to help. Who wouldn't want to share their spiritual gifts at any given opportunity?

But when she got to the birthday party, she saw there was a table set up for her between a clown making balloon animals and a magician. She thought to herself, *Oh, my God, I'm a sideshow act—I'm a dog-and-pony show!*

The point is, you are *not* a circus sideshow act. You have a gift. Not just a talent—a gift! Spiritual gifts are not a novelty. And if you don't treat them with the respect they deserve, no one else will.

Don't be a dog-and-pony show.

Getting in Alignment

We're going to be conscious creators now. It is your birthright to live a full life, be financially abundant, and enjoy yourself while being in alignment with your destiny and feeling the excitement and joy of fulfilling your purpose.

I know, from personal experience, there is nothing more exciting than living your purpose and creating a beautiful life for yourself. It's really a blessing. It is my wish that everyone be able to experience the joy of waking up every morning *knowing* you are doing what Source intended for you.

And you can now know what it feels like, too, with the six simple shifts I am about to teach you, so you can grow your spiritual coaching business to six figures and beyond. All while sharing your message with the world and operating at your highest level of integrity. I'm going to walk you through *exactly* how to make those shifts—starting today.

But first, you may be wondering who I am. If you're

not familiar with me yet, I'm Kimberly Maska, and I am an ex-Wall Streeter and fellow spiritual entrepreneur. Please do not hold the ex-Wall Streeter thing against me. I promise you it is now giving me a great way to serve, and that is why I am here.

I am also the creator of Spiritual Biz Bootcamp and Spiritual Biz Mastery, publisher of *Spiritual Biz Magazine*, and founder of Spiritual Biz Publishing, the publishing company for authors dedicated to shifting consciousness.

We've had some amazing people on the cover of *Spiritual Biz Magazine*, from Sonia Choquette to Colette Baron-Reid, Corey Goode, the Reverend Ed Bacon (who is on Oprah's list of the top one hundred spiritual people on the planet), and Edwene Gaines. Each of them took time to share their stories about how they created financially abundant lives while living their spiritual purpose, so you know it is possible.

I have created this community for people to be able to come together and know they are not alone on their journey as a spiritual entrepreneur. And to know it is not only okay, but necessary to create the energy of money with their spiritual gifts.

Now, a little bit about my story . . .

Let me just say this: My life has always been incredibly magical. I have been able to manifest amazing opportunities and have been truly blessed for how my life has unfolded. I ended up on Wall Street through a series of events that were not specifically planned. But ending up there gave me the unique opportunity to work with eight other partners and to create our own broker dealer (That is just a fancy way of saying we bought and sold securities.).

It was exciting and fun, and we ended up building a $165-million-dollar company. But I knew something was off. Eventually, the fun wore off; I was exhausted. I wasn't sleeping, and my hair was falling out. I was eating too much, and I was drinking too much. Always in this miserable space, I would lie awake every Sunday night dreading work on Monday. The misery set in to such a level I knew I just couldn't do it anymore. But I felt like I was in a marriage with these eight other people because we birthed this company together.

My escape from this misery was to travel, and travel I did; the last I checked, I have been to forty-three countries. Traveling was the only way I could handle the misery I was experiencing. Well, during one of those 'need to escape' modes, I booked a trip to Croatia, where I met a man who is still a dear friend to this day.

He is from New Zealand and, at the time of our meeting, was one of the happiest people I had ever met.

He had been traveling through Europe for months and did not have a job to go back to or even a place to live. In fact, he had left all his belongings with a buddy back home.

This guy was so happy and carefree, yet he didn't have the things that we have been conditioned to link with "happiness." This truly challenged my belief system at the time. He did not have a lot of money, a job, or prestige, but he was in such a great mental state of abundance. We hung out for four days on the beaches of Croatia and then parted ways. When he left, I remember lying on the beach and making the decision to leave Wall Street.

I thought to myself, if I could meet someone who doesn't have the things society equates with success, but who was still that happy—and I am miserable despite my money, my apartment on 5th Avenue, and the ability to travel the world at the drop of a hat—then something is wrong. Really wrong.

I actually called my mom from Croatia and said: "I am quitting my job." My mom reacted with shock because part of her identity was that I was this successful person she could brag to our family about. This was not only a life-changing decision for me, but it was going to have a big impact on her as well. I was leaving behind all the things she had associated with success.

I returned to New York City and really started to think about it. Fear set in. I kept asking myself, "How am I going to make money? Where am I going to live? Stay in N.Y.C.? Move to another country? Go back to L.A.? Would I have to get a normal J.O.B.? I had no clue what I was going to do—I was terrified. It took six months for me to tell my partners I was leaving. Here is a lesson I hope you can learn from: You see, I received inspiration from Source that day in Croatia on the beach. Then my *human* got in the way. My human did all the worrying and hesitating. And what happened? Those six months of hesitation cost me three million dollars.

The infamous downturn of the 2008 U.S. market started to happen. If I had left my company when Source guided me to, I would have received my full pay-out and been living in Paris. Lesson learned.

After I left, I took a year off and went to thirteen countries. I was all over the place—both physically and emotionally—while I figured out what to do.

I bounced around for a bit. I briefly embarked on a stint with a friend's husband to create a music distribution company, but quickly learned that he was more concerned with playing his own music than starting a company.

Then I started flipping houses because I knew real estate, and I knew the numbers. I was not miserable doing this, but I was still not happy. It's a lot of work to flip houses, and sometimes the profit is there and sometimes it isn't. But I was damn good at it! One of my houses even got featured by Yahoo as the best starter home in California (I definitely turned a profit on that one.). However, it was a pain, and it was not really my calling.

Then everything changed when my mom got sick. I was fortunate that I had just closed on three houses. Each had turned a nice profit, so I was able to spend the whole time in the hospital with her.

My Mom's Transition

I don't remember my mom ever being healthy. All my memories are of her being sick and exhausted. She had breast cancer fifteen years before, making her a "survivor," which also meant she was always going to a doctor for check-ups. During one of those check-ups, they discovered that her spleen was enlarged, so she had that removed. Like I said, she was always sick with something.

But this time, I didn't even know she was "sick" until the very end. I would ask about her health, and she would say, "Oh, everything is fine."

It turned out she was lying to me about going to the doctor's. And one day, I was out doing a hundred-mile cycling event, and she was doggy-sitting my adorable pug, Bogart. I had left food at my house for her to eat while she was there. She called me at the event and said, "I think I have food poisoning." However, I had made all the food myself right before I left, so I knew she could not have had food poisoning. It just didn't add up. My intuition was just screaming at me that something was wrong.

She was really sick, so I left immediately and rushed her to the hospital. She was still trying to play everything off like it was no big deal. But the doctors were running around doing more and more tests. I knew this wasn't a good sign, and my mother didn't even look surprised when they told her they found she was riddled with cancer. And I mean *riddled*. Liver, pancreas, lungs, all of her organs.

I tried to unravel what had happened. I needed more answers. Eventually, after making enough phone calls, I found out she had not been going to the doctor like she said she had been. She stopped seeing the doctors when my grandmother transitioned the year before. My grandma was ninety-two—my family line lives a long life if they honor their physical temples and their minds.

Yet here was my mother, who knew she was sick the whole time and lied to me and my dad about it. When it comes down to it, I know what really killed her was all the anger and resentment she had toward the whole family. Unable to let her past go, she carried this anger with her throughout her whole life.

Now, let me back up a little. Five or six months before she got sick, I had been dealing with my own demons. I was still completely unfulfilled with my work, my relationship, everything.

My mom was the one to tell me she thought I was depressed, and of course, all that did was tick me off. I absolutely refused to accept that I was depressed. I couldn't be that person. I had too much going for me to be depressed, right?

But in hindsight, I realize I was. As I came to accept it, I was reading Deepak Chopra's *The Spontaneous Fulfillment of Desire*—the book that changed everything for me. It was the beginning of my whole spiritual journey. And in a moment of divine synchronicity, I flipped to the back of the book where I saw information about his retreats. So, while on my way to a cycling event, I called the number in the book to ask about the retreat and happened to get the very last spot for the next week-long event coming up.

It turned out to be exactly what I needed. I experienced seven days of Ayurvedic detox, meditation, and lots of shedding tears. I came back from that week a completely different person. I had a whole new awareness of me, my life, and how my mother was living—or rather *not* living—her life.

I was also reading Eckhart Tolle, Martha Beck, and Jean Houston at this time. I consumed everything I could get my hands on. I couldn't get enough—it was like this desperate search for answers. Reaching for something I knew was out there but hadn't quite grasped yet.

Shortly after the retreat, my mom got furious at my dad for something minor—I can't even remember what it was. She was yelling and waving her arms—the whole nine yards. I observed her like someone watching a movie when I realized why she was upset and asked her, "Why are you pissed at my dad right now for something that happened to you thirty-five years ago?"

She stopped in her tracks; it was as if I had slapped her right across the face. That was when I realized she didn't even have an awareness of what she was doing.

That comment was the metaphysical slap she needed. I started to coach her through her pain, but that was only four months before she died. And while it didn't really seem like it was enough time, I suppose we never know what happens on someone's deathbed. Those four months of conversations we had could have changed everything for her, and I won't know until I get to the other side myself.

Looking back now, I realize if I hadn't been meditating and reading Deepak, Eckhart, Martha, and Jean, I never would have made it through my mom's transition with my sanity intact. I am an only child, and she was my best friend. This experience was challenging, but my faith that all is as it should be kept me steady.

After she transitioned to the other side, she came for a visit and let me know that she had known the whole time that she had cancer but was too afraid to face her reality. At that moment, I felt relief in knowing she was exactly where she needed to be.

All the information and books I consumed also saved my dad. I taught him how to meditate, and I coached him through his grief. They were married forty-three years; he didn't even know life without my mother. He believes he would have died right after my mom if it hadn't been for his newfound practice of meditation and inner work.

So my thought process at the time was this: If all the information I consumed helped me through her transition, and helped my dad stay present each day, what would it have been able to do for my mom if she had understood all of it before she got sick? What if she had been able to heal her own thoughts, which, in turn, would have healed her own body?

Source has since told me she created her own cancer from being angry and vengeful all the time. She unnecessarily played victim in a lot of ways.

If only she'd had that awareness.

She was an amazing intuitive. She could control the weather like nobody's business. If I was going on a trip, and there was supposed to be a huge storm rolling in, I could just call her, and there would be clear skies the whole way. She was a healer, too. She could touch people and scan them. Then tell them exactly what was wrong in their bodies. But she certainly never felt that was something she could do as a profession.

My mother's transition was the pivotal turning point for my ascension and my career. Because while all this was going on, simultaneously, on my journey of awakening, I started meeting all these people with incredible spiritual gifts. I was already well aware of my impressive manifestation abilities, but when I would talk to these people, I would always get these *tidbits*, causing me to think to myself: *If only I had known that before . . .* or, *If I'd had that little bit of information during . . .*

If you can fix your mind, you can do anything.

So part of my leap into this was wondering: What if this information was more readily available to everyone? What if there was an easy way for people to learn to change their thoughts and, therefore, change their vibrations and course-correct their lives?

If you can fix your mind, you can do anything. When we master our thoughts, we master our reality.

This is Why I do What I do

I am here because I hit complete burnout after co-creating a $165-million-dollar Wall Street firm with eight partners. I am here because my mom wouldn't let go of her past, and it took her life. I am here because, through my own depression, I connected with higher intelligence. And lastly, I am here because while I was on my journey, I met some extraordinarily gifted people just like you. They were struggling. They were struggling with how to get their message out into the world and share their incredible gifts. So now what I've been able to do is use my expertise from my time on Wall Street, all of my business and marketing experience, and my own intuitive gift to be able to "see" someone's business, to show you and other spiritual entrepreneurs how to create financial abundance so that you can serve the world.

When we master our thoughts, we master our reality.

This is my purpose.

I actually *know* this is my soul's purpose because I've had my soul contract done, and I am on my exact path, which is inspiring. You know who read my soul contract? One of those gifted spiritual entrepreneurs I just mentioned. That's my point.

More specifically, it is my purpose to help five thousand spiritual entrepreneurs create five thousand spiritual businesses in the next five years.

Imagine with me. Imagine the paradigm shift that will happen when the healers and lightworkers of the world are thriving financially. Think about the power and the transformation we will have (You felt your chest tighten when you read the word power, didn't you? Breathe.)! It will be unbelievable. I'm still trying to wrap my mind around it; it thrills me to think about it. I'm watching it happen as I help spiritual entrepreneurs step out and have a ripple effect. It's incredible.

Let's hop right into discovering the six key shifts you must make to grow your spiritual business to six figures a year and beyond. This will allow you to share your message with the world while living your purpose. That is why we are here, so I can walk you through all six shifts in this book.

So what are we waiting for?

SHIFT #1
Stop Being Selfish

1
Stop Being Selfish

"The secret to wealth is simple: Find a way
to do more for others than anyone else
does. Become more valuable. Do more.
Give more. Be more. Serve more."

— TONY ROBBINS

THIS FIRST SHIFT is the big one that *really* gets people.
It is *stop being selfish*.

Be honest, "Stop being selfish," triggered you,
didn't it? I know. Bear with me. I will explain.

Think for a moment about the vibration of this
third-density planet we're living on today: Earth. If you
are here with me, right now, then you have awakened.
And you know that there's a massive, worldwide ascen-

sion happening right now.

We can see it all over the place. Everywhere. Just look around.

So that means it's your job, and honestly, your *destiny* as one who's already awakened, to assist with this vibrational shift by helping to change the consciousness on the planet. If you have awakened, you're here to help others awaken as well.

Frankly, you made this agreement before you came in, so we know it's your job and destiny to follow this path. That's why you *must* create a spiritual business now—a really successful one—so that you can get out there and change thousands of lives and have that ripple effect.

But if you're not out there doing it, that means you're not serving anyone, and *you are being selfish*. Yes, it is selfish to withhold your gifts, given to you by Source, from those who need it.

I want to be clear that we're talking about stepping out in a massive way. When I start talking about stepping out, some people get angry and say, "You are letting your ego get in the way, trying to build a tribe." This is a very narrow view of things. No, this is not about your ego; this is about service. Serving as many people as possible, as much as possible. This has nothing to do with you personally, or your ego. This is about service to others around the world.

When you're creating your business, and you're building your tribe, it's not to feed the ego. It's not to get out and have your followers. Or to be looked up to and adored. It's to get out and shift consciousness!

Money is just energy.

This is why I say, "Stop being selfish." If you aren't earning six figures a year (or beyond) as a spiritual coach, then it means you're not influencing enough people. (Or, you are just giving your gifts away for free, so few people are taking you seriously, but we will get to that later.)

This means you're playing small. We have to talk about money; there is no avoiding it. We all obviously need money to survive. But guess what? Money is just *energy*. Let me repeat that. **Money is just energy.** So money is an indicator of how much love you're receiving from your tribe. There is a mandatory energy exchange that must take place.

Let me break it down for you: When you help solve a problem, you are giving energy. When you don't allow energy to come back to you (in the form of money), you are out of balance.

Money is an indicator of how much love you're receiving from your tribe.

The Universe wants everything to be in balance. When things get out of balance, everything goes haywire. We've all been there. It's not pretty.

That means when you're giving and you're serving your clients, you should be open to receiving the energy of money. That is how to hit six figures. If you're not earning six figures, it means you're just not out there. You're not serving enough people, and you haven't set up a real business.

When you're earning six figures, you absolutely know, without a doubt, that you are inspiring thousands of people around the world.

When you don't have that income, that energy exchange, it means you are denying people the chance to experience your gifts. People are praying for the gift you have, and if you're not out there in a big way, you're denying them what they need.

Not only do you deny them of what they need, but you also deny yourself the full expression of you, which is really unfortunate. We have been put on this planet to be the best versions of ourselves. If you aren't living your purpose right now, I need you to step back and really think about this, because you're denying yourself and others your amazing gift.

I'm going to get a bit controversial now. I know one of the things which holds spiritual entrepreneurs back is that they don't want to charge for their services, right? They're afraid to charge for what they're doing because it was a gift from Source.

We've all heard that healers should not get paid and that they should give their gifts away for free. Or, we think that spirituality and money do not belong together. It's like an evil thing if you're charging. I get the most horrendous hate mail and mean comments on my Facebook ads because I'm talking about spirituality and money, which people think is just blasphemous.

I have a theory on why lightworkers have been told to not charge: *I believe it is to keep us down.*

When we are worried and stressed, what happens?

Our focus settles on the problem at hand, which lowers our vibration. It is a challenge to keep our vibration up when we are facing a problem. And they know that. So what better way to keep the healers of the world down than by keeping our vibration low over the stress of money and conditioning us to believe we have to work a job that doesn't feed our souls.

When we are in a low-vibrational state, either from the worry of money or the stress of working a job we can't stand, we are not able to tap into our gifts like we know we can.

We all know that feeling when we're operating in a really high vibration—that things just come to us, and we manifest like crazy. The minute we're worried, everything slows down, and then we struggle, and we're in scarcity mode. It's just not a pleasant place to be.

So I believe that the healers and lightworkers have been told that we should do everything for free to keep us worried and our vibrations low. But could you imagine what the planet would look like if the healers and lightworkers of the world were abundant?

Just think, what would our society be like if all the spiritual people were millionaires!? (And I mean *genuine* spiritual people, people ready to take responsibility for their wealth, not zealots and hypocrites.)

If we were abundant, we wouldn't be worrying about things. Because when we are abundant, things are easily solved. A thousand-dollar car repair is not an emergency; it is a simple fix. Plus, we would be able to manifest and create in unbelievable ways. Having abundance means we can be the best version of ourselves, and we can provide service to others.

Imagine if the Fortune 500 companies were all serving and shifting consciousness as well. What would that be like? The world that we know today would be unrecognizable. All the negative energy would start to dissipate because the people with the beautiful vision to raise the vibration of the planet would be out there helping to shift consciousness.

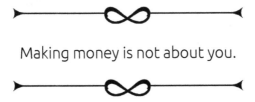

Making money is not about you.

Now, going back to money, because I know this is such a button-pusher for people. I want to be clear about one thing:

Making money is not about you.

This is not about you making all sorts of money and

going out and buying a bunch of stuff. There's a lot of nonsense that people buy. Our houses are full of things we don't need. That is *not* what I'm talking about.

What I *am* talking about is being able to give back. When we're in a place of financial abundance, we can freely give that abundance away, and when we can do that, we create a ripple effect on this planet. (I know, I mention this ripple effect a lot. But get used to it because it is *important.* I am definitely not done talking about it.) We're able to take our financial abundance and share it with others. At the end of the day, it isn't about how much we make or even how much we keep, it is about how much we give away.

Let's take a look at this a little bit deeper, so we're all on the same page. Let's say you make $40,000 a year, and you are tithing (or *want* to tithe). Now, when I talk about tithing, which means to donate 10 percent of your gross income, I'm not talking about to a church only. It could be a church, or it could be any organization you feel compelled to share your energy with.

There is always this confusion around tithing. What does it really mean? It has this kind of old, antiquated, even negative connotation. But I want to shift that. It's a new time, a new age, and there is a new way of thinking.

Tithing is about an energy exchange with the Universe. Allowing energy to flow out and flow in. When we do so, it builds momentum and power (there is that word again). But when your money isn't flowing, it becomes stagnant. You *need* it to flow out in order to flow back in. Like the flow of a river. When the water is not flowing, it becomes stagnant, gross, attracts flies. When you are just taking and taking and taking and then spending on *things,* there's a stagnation of money.

When people are in scarcity mode, they tend not to tithe. They hang on tight to every cent because fear and scarcity are controlling them. The irony is that when you are really in a state of, "Oh, no! Where did my money go? I need more *now!*" that is the *exact* time you need to be tithing.

Hear me out here. I know it sounds scary. But whenever I get myself in a quandary where I'm thinking the money isn't coming in, and I start to get nervous, I just go give a bunch away. Seriously. It helps every time.

One of my students heard me say this once, and she was actually at a spiritual retreat with her Guru at that moment. She literally went downstairs to the lobby of the hotel where the retreat check-in was and donated the remaining balance on her credit card—$15,000—because that was 10 percent of her income goal for the year. She wanted to show her faith that she would make that amount in the year, so she tithed in advance. Now, that is some serious trust in the Universe right there. But the Universe delivered. She made that money back within a week, and then some. And if you're wondering whether she made that income goal, yes, she most certainly did. She actually made more. So she was able to give even more away.

And I remember a time, not that long ago, when I was still working to get Maska Media flowing like I had envisioned, and I was down to my very last $100. I had no idea how I was going to pay my rent or where the next check was coming from (I was still working with clients one-on-one.). I heard a clear message, "Give it away." So I did, to a church that had a message I loved, and the rest is history.

Begin to tithe, and show the Universe, God, Source, whichever name resonates with you, that you have complete faith that all of your needs will be met. Faith that the Universe will allow it to flow back in. Resist the urge to sit in scarcity mode, where you are focused on the negative. This will energetically suffocate your bank account.

So what is tithing, really? Traditionally, it means giving the church 10 percent of your income. But when

I'm talking about it here, that's not really what I'm saying. But kind of. Let me explain.

You want to give your money to a cause that shares the message you believe in. If it's an institution of love that's raising consciousness, and that feels good to you, then that needs to be where your money goes. Your money should flow to where you are being spiritually fed.

Technically, it should be 10 percent. That's the definition of *tithe*. But that scares some people, and tithing has to feel *good*. Ten percent has been one of those Universal laws for a long time to keep the flow going. Back in the day, people used to give 10 percent of their crops so they would have abundance the following years. So historically, yes, 10 percent.

But, if you are giving away the money, and you're complaining and moaning about it the whole time, then that's not the time to do it. You have to feel good about it! You have to be in alignment with sharing the money and allowing it to flow out to support a message or a cause.

Now, let's talk about what tithing is *not*.

Tithing is *not* giving to family members or giving handouts to homeless people on the street. Not that there's anything wrong with that. I'm just saying, it's not tithing.

When we talk about giving money away, it needs to be a hand *up* and not a hand*out*; it is about donating to institutions and nonprofits that are there to help people raise up their lives.

It also has to be a situation where you're not getting a direct benefit from it. If you purchase something from an organization for yourself, or you give to your kids' school, that doesn't count.

It's free giving! Have faith it will come back. What flows out will flow in. Trust. And remember, when in big-time scarcity . . . give it away. Something even better will flow back to you.

One of the best parts is that when you do it consistently, you will see the rewards. It's an incredible feeling. You want to see your bank account grow? Start giving money away. I'm serious.

Now, back to our example, let's say you're making $40,000 a year, and you donate 10 percent of your income, that's a lovely $4,000. But here's the thing, if you have a family, kids, a mortgage, and a car payment, I bet you're barely scraping by on $40,000. So you're probably not donating the 10 percent you could be giving back to the planet because things are really tight. Am I right?

Now, let's say you created your amazing spiritual business, and you are hitting the six-figure mark. If you make $100,000 or more, and then you freely give 10 percent (or more) of that income back into the world, now you're contributing $10,000 to the Universal flow of money. That's amazing!

Think of how many more families you can feed, how many more puppies you can save (if animals are your love), or school supplies you can buy for children in third-world countries with the extra $6,000 you donate (or maybe it's the full $10,000 because you might not have been giving anything at all before).

Do you see now why you must be crossing the six-figure mark? Why you must be charging for your gift? Why you must be out there in a big way? Think about how fulfilling your life will be when you are touching thousands of lives on a daily basis instead of just a few dozen or the few family members who come to you for advice and guidance.

Imagine the *ripple effect*.

It's really no longer an option to play small. We have to shift the vibration of this planet, and we have to do it *now*. No more playing small. No more letting your ego get in your head, saying you're afraid and letting all the fear stuff come up. It is time to realize this has nothing to do with you. This has to do with service to others. It has to do with raising the vibration of the planet and the people around you.

Let me tell you about Stacie. She did it, and so can you. Stacie is an angelic psychic medium; she had a near-death experience. After that experience, she was gifted with the ability to connect with angels. She's phenomenal. She blows me away with what she does.

When she came to me, she was working her tail off doing one-off sessions. And she was charging $78 an hour, which, if you're familiar with my philosophies, you know that this number is totally not acceptable. Your gift is worth much more than that.

Together, we restructured her business, and she created her Soul Solution course. When she launched it, within two weeks of the launch, she had eight new clients enrolled in her program. She came out with a beta-test price of $950. With that $950 price, she created $7,600 in two weeks. And she has more people joining her program every week.

She was able to make the shift and see that by playing small, she wasn't really serving. Now her clients write her these beautiful notes and testimonials saying how their lives have been completely transformed because she stepped out in a big way. She is now changing thousands of lives around the world. It's an incredible thing, and *you can do this, too.*

When I asked Stacie how she found me, she didn't even remember. But she knew she felt very pulled to work with me. Everything aligned to draw us together, and it just felt right, for both of us.

In my Spiritual Biz Bootcamp program, Stacie was determined to make her money back ASAP—and she sure did. Fast. I helped her shift her thinking from meeting with people one at a time was the best way to serve; it's not. She went from working with people live and in person to setting up a program so she wasn't working all the time (and telling people the same things over and over). This gave her more time with her family, and to travel, and really serve at a high level. Plus, she could reach a *lot* more people.

Stacie also got to meet a spiritual book editor in Bootcamp, who helped her finish her inspirational book of angel channelings along with her story of her cancer journey—the story Stacie had wanted to publish for four years but never knew how. She also dealt with some fear around releasing such a spiritually focused book into her conservative world, but we will go into that more in a minute. The book is called *Angel Kisses: No More Cancer,* and, I'm proud to say, it was released in April of 2019.

Like me, Stacie came from corporate America, so she resonated with my style and background—plus the spiritual side of me. We shared the whole empath/no-nonsense parts of our personalities.

Stacie came from a Christian background initially, but then she was torn after her incredible near-death experience. When we met, she was coming to a new place in life—a place of wanting to be a spiritual teacher. Because she had battled cancer, watched her husband pass away (They actually battled together, but he transitioned, and she didn't.), and was able to see the angels as they showed up around his deathbed, she knew she wanted to do more. She had become a whole new person.

Before that, she was in church all the time; she spoke there and went to Bible study. Now, these experiences she was having were supposedly not okay, of the "dark side" even.

But Stacie knew she wasn't dabbling on the dark side. She also wasn't asking for these things to happen. And although she thought she was crazy at first, and didn't know how to explain any of it, she could feel in her heart that it was a spiritual gift from Source. A gift she couldn't ignore.

She started to meet some other sensitives who experienced the same types of things as she did and finally had confirmation that she wasn't crazy. She worked with a mentor to dial in her spiritual gifts, and it validated her, but she wanted more. She *needed* more. So she relocated out into the country, in the middle of nowhere, where she felt like a monk on a mountain. She spent all this time alone just painting and sitting in nature. Turning the world off for six whole months. Finally, she realized she was channeling these angel messages through the colors and shapes she painted. That's when she knew she had to practice with other people.

Practicing via distance for free is how she started. Phone call, Skype, you name it. And this was extremely successful. When she felt ready, she moved into being paid, but, like I said earlier, she was only charging $78 per reading. And this wasn't just for her hour-long reading; oh, no, she spent an hour beforehand preparing to hold space for them, writing, channeling, tuning in. She said she would get on the phone with these people and sometimes just talk for the full sixty minutes without letting them say a word. Then, at the end, when sixty minutes were up, she would just blurt out, "Okay, thanks. Bye!" She laughs when she talks about this now. She said it was weird, but thought to herself, *Holy cow! Did that just happen?*

The testimonials came pouring in. She was changing people's lives, and they were grateful, but she knew she could still give them more. She wasn't giving enough or spending enough time with the client to understand their deepest wounds and needs. A one-off, hour-long phone call was great and all, but it wasn't enough.

She was being selfish without even realizing it. By trying to be self*less*, and not wanting to charge them too much, she was being self*ish* by not giving them the full extent of her gifts. She was also being selfish by not charging enough. The clients weren't valuing her or themselves at $78 an hour.

But she didn't even know where to start. She knew she needed to set up programs to bless lives on an ongoing basis, but how? She needed to be deeply involved with them so she could guide them to profound healing. But what did that look like?

That is where I came in. During my Spiritual Biz Bootcamp, she learned systems and technical aspects to streamline her business. This changed her profoundly because it has allowed her to shift her whole perspective about spirituality, money, and business.

She now understands she is part of the next wave, leading a new wave of lightworkers to step up and be leaders themselves. These souls are healing with every step they take without even saying a word. People just know there is something about them. That's how they are creating a ripple effect and continuing that ripple effect on and on for eternity. What a gift!

Her gift continues to keep on giving. At the time of this writing, which is two years after we started working together, she brought in $12,000 in sales just in a month. She is changing lives every day with her program. She's no longer doing the work *for* them. She's giving them the tools to heal on a deep soul level so they can serve as a light-being themselves. Single sessions are a thing of the past. Plus, she is running her own spiritual retreats. Her spiritual business has evolved so much since we first met over two years ago, her six-figure spiritual business is her new norm.

She is proud to be reigniting the light for her clients. The lights that had previously been snuffed out. Because of Stacie, they are sparkling once again and getting brighter. She sees it every day. Her clients look happier and feel lighter and brighter. She is proud to be such a big part of their journeys. And I am proud to be a part of hers. Stacie inspires me, and it is an honor to be with her along the way.

"Kimberly helped me get the systems in place to start the momentum, now I *WING* it!" ~Stacie

Begin your energy exchange with the Universe today with my Tithing Plan. My free gift to you. Get it here: www.areyouaspiritualentrepreneur.com.

SHIFT #2
Marrying
Spirituality and Money

2
Marrying
Spirituality and Money

"Money is a symbol of God's opulence, beauty, refinement, and abundance, and it should be used wisely, judiciously, and constructively to bless humanity in count-less ways."

— DR. JOSEPH MURPHY

SO, FOR SHIFT number two, we're talking about spiri-tuality and money. Is it an oxymoron? This is the funni-est thing because I actually get this written on my ads all the time: "Spirituality and money is an oxymoron."

But it's not. Let's take a look at this misconception.

As I said, I hear this all the time. This might have

even been your first thought when you read the title of the chapter. It's been so deeply ingrained in us, it feels like it is a true statement. Do you sometimes wonder if it's true? Are you thinking, "Is it really okay to charge for my spiritual gifts?"

I understand why there might be some confusion, but that just means that we really haven't opened up our minds much.

I would like you to ponder this for a second: Why is it okay to make money when we are completely out of alignment with Source? Why is it "okay" for major corporations to turn a profit by selling us poisoned food, but it is not okay to make money from your spiritual gifts? Something is amiss.

Are you going to a job that you can't stand every day? Are you putting up with coworkers who constantly test your patience? Why? For money? For money that has been tainted with a low vibration of misery?

We have all done it at some point in our lives. We go to work, day in and day out, like sheeple. It's the golden handcuffs scenario. We work for money and pay for it with our happiness, and sometimes our lives.

The issue is that money you make from the job you don't like is never satisfying because it feels like you had to give something up in order to receive it. You have to *deal* with a nasty boss. You have to *deal* with a long commute. You have to *deal* with getting up early and all the nonsense that happens with a regular job.

I remember what that was like. I'm so grateful I don't have to do that anymore. What happens when you work an unsatisfying job is that you end up feeling like you're owed something. At the end of the week, you worked so hard, and have been so miserable, that you start to look for a quick "fix" so you can feel good again. You take your money, and you go shopping and buy something you probably don't need just because you want to reward yourself for the hard week. As you are making a purchase you know you don't need, or throwing back one too many beers, you say to yourself, "I deserve this," because of the wretched work week you had to endure.

I remember during my Wall Street years I had an unusually miserable day. I honestly couldn't tell you what made that day stand out, but I can clearly see myself leaving the building and stepping out onto 5th Ave in frustration.

Our office was in Rockefeller Center, and if you have ever been to New York City, you know that means you are only steps from Saks Fifth Avenue and every luxury designer store you can imagine. I headed north and somehow ended up in Fendi. I was so blind with anger from the day that I don't even remember walking to the store. But when I stepped in, there was a sense of relief, a *knowing* that something in that store could make me "feel" better.

I spotted a beautiful handbag, and just touching it relieved some of my anger. I didn't even look at the price tag, just plopped it on the counter. I am actually embarrassed to share this story, because that handbag cost me $3,500. Stupid. Just stupid. Who could I have truly helped with that money? But I share my experience because there is a lesson here.

Whether it is a $3,500 handbag or that fifth pair of shoes that look just like the rest of the ones in your closet that still have price tags on them, or that third martini that you should have said no to, we know deep in our souls that these things are just signs that something is wrong in our lives. Pay attention to the signs.

The money that we make when we're out of alignment is never satisfying. It can't be. It is tainted. That means the only way you should be making money is by living your purpose, by being in alignment with Source and serving others. That is how we become fulfilled, and I can tell you from personal experience it feels really good to create an income that way.

I promise you, income generated from a place of full alignment and service to others is going to be far greater than anything you've ever worked for.

If your primary source of income isn't via your spiritual business, then you are really compromising your core agreement with Source Energy. Sit with that for a little bit. When you agreed to come into this density, you had a plan. There is a role for you to play, a purpose you were sent here to fulfill. Each of us has a unique purpose, but ultimately it comes down to being the best version of ourselves and being of service to others when you're here on this planet. Is it time to make a change so you can really live your purpose? If you're reading this sentence, then I can only guess that the answer is yes.

Now, I'm going to talk to you about Natie and Javier, a couple who found me on an Abraham-Hicks cruise. They heard about what I was doing, and they were interested in learning more.

Let me tell you, watching them flourish has been a beautiful sight to behold. They are shifting mindsets around spirituality and money left and right, and they're doing it in *Latin America!* I love this.

When they found me, they had just moved from Ecuador to Mexico and knew they needed to take the next step in their spiritual business. Nati trusted me immediately because we came from the same latin background (I am half Mexican and half Czechoslovakian.). She got super engaged with my message.

They both jumped right into my Spiritual Biz Bootcamp program with few questions asked. This was September of 2017. At the time, they already had a business that wasn't necessarily *un*successful, but they knew they could take it much further. They believed in the Law of Attraction, and they trusted it. They knew the Law of Attraction brought them to me, after all.

At the time, Natie was already walking around saying, "I am a six-figure woman!" And she believed it with her whole self. But Javier; he admits he wasn't quite there yet. But they had each other. And they believed in each other. And once again, I believed in them.

They shared how important it was for them to work together as a team. Together, they live in a mental state where their success is expected. Continually. They trust the Law of Attraction will bring the perfect clients to them, and this is certainly the case. It's part of the process itself. When the relationship works, it all works. Everything works!

Part of their process is connecting to each other each day. They have a schedule, but otherwise, they allow the Law of Attraction to bring them the right souls. And now the business that they teach and love is what saved their lives. And it is saving the lives of others. There's that ripple effect again.

They make a point of nourishing their relationship and having fun together with what they do. They even do a romantic couples' getaway for one weekend every month. Relationship maintenance is directly correlated to business maintenance. Especially now that they can finally afford to take care of themselves.

Before Bootcamp, they were bringing in between $2,000 and $2,500 per month with their spiritual business. They already had a social media page with 300,000 followers, but it didn't monetize. They knew they had something great, but weren't entirely sure what to do with it yet.

Their business has certainly evolved. Before, they say it was more like a hobby. They had a lot of followers but very few clients. And most of these clients were only looking for one session at a time. When they came to work with me, their goal was to make between $3,000 and $4,000 per month.

Everything started to change when we began to

co-create together. I wanted them to see they could achieve even more than they could currently imagine. They were truly changing lives! But their decision to succeed was really what made the difference. They *chose* to be successful. They *allowed* success. And people noticed. Their whole vibrations changed. Fifteen months later, the result has been unbelievable. They are making between $18,000 and $25,000 per month—when their goal was only three or four!

Javier even says, "Now, if I build it, people come. It's so different from how it was before." He also says, "But *you* have to do the work yourself! No one else will take over and do it for you."

They teach this concept to the masses now, and it's working. It's working really well. People are saying their lives are changing when they work with this incredible couple, and they're telling all their friends.

What exactly do Natie and Javier do? They use real-life experience to help people understand how the Law of Attraction works. To allow their clients to see how LOA works in their own lives. Natie admits that's only what they tell their clients, but in the background what they are really doing is working with their shadows. They help people learn how to tell a new story, raise their vibrations, and believe in themselves.

Eventually, it becomes easy to look at all aspects of the shadows—they have done this work themselves with great success. This is how Natie and Javier are able to help others do it on such a raw and authentic level.

Javier says that when he looks back, he knows they are so good now because things were so bad. It has allowed them to learn from their pasts and processes. They know that when they finally got out of their own way, and allowed the Universe to step in, everything fell into place. It saved their lives, and it's what they teach.

Their students even wonder how things just suddenly start to work out. But Natie and Javier smile and admit they just "trick" them into doing it themselves.

In July of 2018, the couple brought in $18,000. But then they started to wobble. They felt guilty about having so much money. Then scarcity mindset set in. They started to think, *I can't handle this!* So the following month, their income dropped down to $9,000, then $7,000. They admitted to bringing it on themselves, and they knew they needed to get their mindsets back in the right place. Immediately, the numbers popped right back up to $25,000. So they are a fantastic living example of trusting the Universe and allowing the ebb and flow. When you allow, the flow increases.

In February of 2019, their understanding of the ebb and flow made them decide to join my Spiritual Biz Mastery program. Now I get to work with them on a more intimate level and see the global impact they're having.

When I ask them what they still struggle with, they admit the balance of the amount of money you want with the amount of time you want for yourself can be tricky. But how do you make the most money with less time? A fantastic question for any spiritual entrepreneur. Sometimes we work so hard to get everything going, and we get lost in it.

But the thing that made them so successful was their determination to follow Bootcamp to the T. They say they would look around in Bootcamp at the others, and some of them weren't doing the outer or inner work. Javier admits that Natie was the one who studied hard and did every single step I outlined in Bootcamp. She trusted, and it opened Javier's eyes. He quickly saw the difference between the others who were having success and those who weren't. The ones who weren't actually following the steps and focusing their attention were struggling (read "self-sabotage" into this). But watching others succeed, now that inspired him. Where some might be jealous of watching others succeed, Nati and Javier allowed themselves to be inspired and set the course for their own forward motion.

They *chose* success.

Natie and Javier *knew* they would make it, so they did. But having each other balanced them out. This has been a healing journey for both of them and will continue to be so.

It was beautiful to watch Nati get choked up as she talked about her journey. She said she wanted to invest in herself and in the world. "It allows you to be yourself and shed what you don't need anymore."

Her next focus is writing her book because she knows the book will make a difference. Are you noticing a theme here?

If you aren't earning 6 figures yet, your money story might need to be upgraded. My free gift to you, a Money Story exercise. Get it here: www.areyouaspiritualentrepreneur.com.

SHIFT #3
The Secret Weapon

3
The Secret Weapon

"Being rich is having money; being wealthy
is having time."

— Margaret Bonnano

NOW WE'RE ON to shift number three, the secret
weapon. This is one of my favorites, so stick with me if
I get a little riled up. This is fun.

The secret weapon for creating the freedom you
desire in your business is what I call, *Making Money While You Meditate™*. I love that. It's so simple, it
sounds too good to be true, right?

Making Money While You Meditate™; what does
that mean?

It means generating *passive income* in a beautiful way

that still helps the world. And the energy you put forth into your business from the meditation itself (and even having time to meditate) feeds your soul and the global vibration all at once.

It allows you to connect with your tribe, share your knowledge on a global level, and create financial abundance without the mental exhaustion you experience when working one-on-one with clients. We all know how exhausting it can be when you're with clients all day long, and they're rescheduling, or they just don't show up. I know you're trying to keep your business organized, but when you are depending on other people to show up, it can be a real mess. We're going to look at a better way, but first, let's review the old way.

The old way consists of going out "there" (wherever "there" might be, your community, your website, social media) and searching and searching for clients. You look for clients everywhere. You have a slick-looking website. You attend Meetups. You post daily on Facebook. After spending a lot of energy searching for a client, you find an interested party. You chat with them a little bit, and they agree to work with you. They finally say, "Yes, I want you to help me."

Then you book some time with them, and after spending an hour or more with them, they pay you.

Here's the problem: When you connect your time with money, it really limits your cash flow.

It leads to burnout because if you want to increase your income, you have to work more hours. There are only so many hours in the day, so you can only make so much money at a time. At some point, you need to sleep and eat and spend time with your family. It's really exhausting.

Now the new way: Making Money While You Meditate™. Here's the idea: You can check your bank account in the morning, then you meditate, spend time with your family, do whatever it is that you desire to do. When you come back and check later, you have more money in your bank account than you did when you started off.

Doesn't that sound lovely? It really is cool, and I know I love it every time I have money coming in while I am out having dinner with my husband. My time isn't tied to my income.

Let's look at the new way in a little bit more detail. So here's the concept: You create a program, then an *online* program. You automate it, and you advertise it out into the world. You advertise it out to your tribe, who resonates with it, connects with it, and makes a purchase.

The key to this whole process is "advertising." When someone is treating their business as a hobby, they seem to skip the advertising piece and rely solely on the Law of Attraction. Advertising is what shifts your business from a hobby to a true business.

Advertising, when used in conjunction with the Law of Attraction, is an incredible tool. It allows you to connect with your tribe in ways that just aren't possible if you are stuck looking in your community for clients. With advertising, you can have a global reach.

And as I mentioned before, when you automate your programs, your income isn't tied to your time, so you can actually have more time to serve others. You can dedicate your time elsewhere, whether serving others means volunteering at a hospital or spending more time with your loved ones. You're able to serve in a greater way because you have more time and still have money-energy coming in.

Still sounds too good to be true? There is one catch. Automation just doesn't work if you do not have a deep soul connection with your tribe. To be able to connect intimately with your tribe is a skill. A skill that took me a few good "failures" to figure out.

In the very beginning of my business, I had this brilliant idea; I would create a ten-module automated course to show spiritual entrepreneurs how to launch their business. It was called Jump Start Your Spiritual Business. After two solid months of creating slide decks, recording modules, editing videos, setting up my email sequences and building a webinar, I was ready.

I had over 3,000 followers in my Facebook Group, about the same number on my professional page, and an email list that was 2,000 strong. I crunched the numbers and estimated that at least thirty people would buy my program. The price point? $997 or twelve payments of $97. My mind was awhirl with a $30,000 payday.

The webinar date was set, and the Facebook ads began to run (I had a $1,500 budget for advertising.). Every time someone signed up for the webinar my heart did a little dance. This was exciting stuff!

Finally, the day arrived for the live webinar. About forty people attended live, and it was exhilarating to know that forty people were listening to *me* talk. Yup, my ego was thoroughly enjoying the attention. When it was done, I felt like I nailed the webinar. I told them exactly what they needed to hear.

Now, I would liken the moments after a live webinar as to what it might feel like when you have been nominated for Best Actress at the Academy Awards. It is exciting but nerve-wracking. I took a sip of water and checked my email for the "You Have Money" email we all wait for. Nothing. "Hmm . . . okay, I will give them some time to read the sales page and put their credit card information in," I thought. I checked back fifteen minutes later. Nothing.

Then I realize, oh, wait, they say most people don't show up live, that is why your email sequence is so important. So I waited. The first purchase came a day after the webinar. Then another and another. Then crickets. That was it. Three purchases. It was a fraction of what I had calculated. And the worst part? They all took the $97 a month option, so my income from that webinar was less than $300. I was devastated.

I had put two months of my energy into creating something I *knew* they needed. I told them exactly what they needed to hear on the webinar, and I had spent my last dollars on this launch. That story I told earlier about tithing my last $100? Yeah, it was right after this lesson.

So, why didn't they buy?

Because I had no connection with my tribe. They didn't know me, and frankly, I didn't really know them. I was teaching what I *thought* they needed, making it all about me. Huge mistake.

This was a wake-up call for me to find that deep, intimate connection with the souls that know me. That is a big part of what I teach my clients now, and I see it work every time.

So, only after you have a soul connection with your tribe can you Make Money While You Meditate™. And when you put this in place, you will be able to reach a greater audience, with price points for everyone. Your tribe will have a way to connect with you and learn from you. This will lead to more income, more money-energy, to share with the world.

So here is another successful shift. David Strickel channels a group of entities which call themselves the Stream. He is a powerful channel who helps people overcome abundance blocks, health issues, and just their own negative self-talk and limiting beliefs. He came to me through another one of my students, Qat Wanders (You will hear more about her when we get to shift number five.). At this time, he already had a popular podcast, *The Stream of David*, but wasn't yet bringing in any income with his spiritual business. Having just finished writing a book, he was searching for a spiritually focused book editor. He hired Qat.

In the process of working together, David mentioned he was looking for a spiritual business coach to help him grow his business into a full-time income. Qat suggested he talk to her mentor (me) and arranged a video call for us to see if we were a fit.

The funny part about it was that our initial phone call did *not* go smoothly! I could feel David's resistance coming up during our conversation. He said he didn't want some cookie-cutter program, and he looked down on online courses because of his previous biases. I cut the phone call short, sending him on his way, but told him to consult the Stream about it and to come back if he changed his mind. I certainly didn't want to let him into Spiritual Biz Bootcamp if he wasn't a good fit.

Well, apparently, the Stream had other plans and guided him right back to me. This *was* the path he needed to be on, and the intention was for him to go deeper than the Law of Attraction and the Abraham method. If you are at all familiar with Abraham-Hicks, you know they were the driving force behind opening people up to the message of the Law of Attraction (LOA)—but the Stream wants us all to know there is more to the story. For David, learning my methods and doing the course was the path to lasting positive change in people's lives.

When I brought him into my program, everything immediately resonated with him. It was overwhelming at first, and there was a lot for him to learn. This was a hard pill for him to swallow because he had always been self-taught. He didn't get past the tenth grade; he got his GED, taught himself to shave, to tie a tie, swim, but the Stream clearly told him he needed to be taught. In this case, he had to step back, let go, embrace it, and "drink the Kimberly Kool-Aid." (Seriously, those are the Stream's words, not mine!)

David set the positive intention from the get-go to do all of it and to have a successful outcome. To this day, I believe he is the only one to have completed literally everything I teach in Spiritual Biz Bootcamp in the allotted time. In fact, he completed the entire program in twelve weeks while dealing with a major health crisis in his life and even moved from San Francisco to Palm Springs.

Looking back, David says he now knows this was exactly what he needed. The Stream knew it all along, it just took him a little bit to stop arguing and listen. He earned $60,000 directly from the program just in the twelve weeks he was in Bootcamp. He told me he set the intention from the beginning to earn back his investment, and he did so many times over! He has since even brought another friend to me who has now surpassed him in income during the twelve weeks.

After graduating Bootcamp, David promptly joined my Spiritual Biz Mastery program. He has grown his business exponentially. The course he initially produced has evolved into what he calls Tya Bootcamp and a separate Tya Academy. Tya is the shortened term for "Trust Your Abundance," and it is the core of what the Stream teaches. The Stream of David has created a spiritual practice—the next evolution of LOA—to change lives worldwide.

They teach us to shed the need for tools and modalities of religion, structured practices, and traditions, so we can harness the power of our own creative abilities.

Eight months out of the program, David has brought in $157,000 in income just using the tools I taught him. The best part? He has streamlined all of this using these methods. So he literally makes money while he meditates. How's that for creating your own abundance?

Ready to automate? There is a secret to pricing your automated programs. Discover the secret here: www.areyouaspiritualentrepreneur.com.

SHIFT #4
See Your Business as a Vehicle to Serve

4

See Your Business as a Vehicle to Serve

"Allow your passion to become your purpose, and it will one day become your profession."

— GABRIELLE BERNSTEIN

NOW LET'S HOP into shift number four, seeing your business as a vehicle to serve. So every day I hear (literally, every day) from what I call spiritual "wantrepreneurs." That might offend a few, but most of them are, and, well, as an awakened individual, nothing should offend you anyways. Spiritual "wantrepreneurs" have a hobby, and they haven't put the necessary energy into it to turn it into a real business. That's a clear definition of a "wantrepreneur."

They tell me they want to "help people," but they aren't taking any of the necessary steps to really serve on this planet.

Many of them have spent countless hours, over many years, honing their spiritual modalities. They have studied with gurus, traveled to sacred sites around the world, focusing on mastering meditation is part of their daily routine, and they are doing all of this in the name of serving and helping people.

They are true masters in their modalities, but the energy they have put into their spiritual business is practically zero. The spiritual knowledge to spiritual business ratio is completely out of balance. So, how are they helping the people if they have all of that knowledge and spiritual insight, but they are not sharing it? Exactly my point, they are not.

Think about the last retreat you went to or the person you've studied with who really transformed your life. What would've happened if you had never heard of that person? The only reason you found them is because they gathered their courage, overcame their fears, and stepped out as a spiritual leader. Kudos to them.

So if you have gifts to give and knowledge to share, then the time has come for you to get your message out there, too.

Without a spiritual business, you're making a half-hearted attempt at genuinely serving.

If you really want to serve, if you really want to help people, which is what every spiritual entrepreneur says, well, then you need to build your spiritual business.

Your spiritual business is the vehicle in which you can serve and help thousands around the world. Without a spiritual business, you're making a half-hearted attempt at genuinely serving.

You're really being selfish because you have all these amazing gifts and knowledge, yet you're keeping them to yourself. I don't think that's what Source had in mind when you were given these gifts. You were given gifts to share, to serve others, to shift consciousness on the planet.

So if you're one of those people who wants to help people, you must have a *vehicle*, and that vehicle to *serve* with is your *spiritual business.*

You can tell how passionate I am about this because this is how we're going to create that ripple effect I keep mentioning. It is time for you to overcome any self-limiting beliefs that are holding you back and step up *now* so together we can change consciousness and shift the vibration of the planet.

Here is another one of my awesome clients stepping out to serve. Her name is Brigette. Brigette's soul-purpose is to provide people with the opportunity to connect with their inner guidance.

She knew it was time to play big. She knew this because she was playing really, really small. She had only made $2,000 in an entire year with her spiritual business. She *knew* she was done playing really small, so she made the decision to step out and serve her clients in a big way.

We shifted a few things in her business and beliefs, and just with that initial shift—we didn't even have her course done yet—she was instantly booked thirty days out. It was unbelievable. She earned $7,800 in a month. This was before we even got her course out!

Brigette had a lot to say about her transformation, which was phenomenal to witness. When she found me in early 2017, she had been searching for a mentor for some time. But every time she would look into working with one, there would be some kind of missing component.

When we talked, she said it wasn't about the money; it was about the feeling inside her body she knew she would get when she found the right person. When she listened to my webinar, she knew I was the one who lined up with her spiritual connection.

She realized that she had been trying to do it all by herself. That is a slow and tedious process, trying to build a business with no support. Brigette knew that, to get things done at a faster pace so she could best serve her family and herself, she needed help. Help from someone who could take her to the next level. It was time to dive in with a mentor.

At first, she was even afraid to talk to her husband about the whole thing because they were struggling financially. But she held her ground because she had been asking, "Where is this mentor?" over and over. And even though she had major resistance, she held herself accountable. She even told her husband, "I can't miss this chance! I'm gonna take it!"

Her husband was so scared because they were on food stamps and have three little boys, but Brigette knew, deep in her heart, this was the golden ticket. And, sooner than expected, her husband ended up being in alignment with it, too. Fully supportive, he said to her, "Just don't leave me behind."

How sweet is that?

Still, Brigette expressed lots of discomfort while she was growing into her new self. She even said, "By working with someone who was so solid in who she was, it mirrored back the points where I wasn't showing up for myself."

The program gave her the opportunity to be vulnerable in a space full of people who didn't run away from her. She said that before, when she shined her light, people would leave her and be afraid. This, in turn, made *her* afraid of her own light.

But working with others who surrounded her with real and unconditional love was an experience people talk about but don't always get. This was new for her. She got to shine her light around others who shined just as brightly. "It mirrored back so much it allowed me to love myself enough so I could take the steps to do what my heart really wanted," says Brigette.

Brigette is now living her best life and agrees Spiritual Biz Bootcamp was the vehicle that got her there.

When I challenged her to bring in $10,000 a month, it made her show up for *herself*. This challenged her to believe it was possible. I knew she could do it, and I helped her see herself and her gift through my eyes. The eyes that saw her as worthy and deserving.

With her newfound confidence, she went out and started serving as Source had intended—and it was about time! After hiding behind her gifts for so long, she found herself in a community where she witnessed others serving as well. This amplified everything for her because it showed her what was possible.

As stated earlier, Brigette went from a total income of $2,000 in 2016 to over $20,000 in 2017 (and that was in only six months). In 2018, she stepped it up again and joined my Spiritual Biz Mastery program. She brought in $116,000 that year by using her gifts to help people change their lives!

Her gifts haven't just served her clients either. They have served her family in a big way also. She sent her children to a Montessori school (She had wanted to do this for years but couldn't afford it.). Her husband was able to quit his job. She even hired her little sister full-time as a nanny (abundance for the whole family!), allowing her sister to start her own business.

Brigette finally has the extra personal power

and energy to extend out to others around her. This is something she never had before. She felt like she would always have to do everything herself. Now, her nearest and dearest have benefited, so she gets to see the fruits of her labor up close on a daily basis.

If you are wondering, "What exactly does Brigette do?" here is her answer:

"Using emotional intelligence, I assist people with reprogramming their subconscious minds so they can create new patterns in their reality. In my program, we tap into the sexual energy and vulnerability in the individual so they can use it to extend out into their relationships—like I have been able to do."

I get chills just reading over that.

Her original course, which she priced at $3,000, is going on autopilot so she can make money while she meditates. Brigette now also takes her clients into a six-month mastery program of her own. The first three months consist of deep self-exploration and acceptance. The next three months focus on being able to hold that space for others.

But it all started with that twelve-week program, Spiritual Biz Bootcamp. She wants others to know that this program is for the person ready to make life work *for* them instead of letting life happen *to* them. She says, "Life works for you; you don't work for life. We have been programmed to think that way. Bootcamp helps you realize that."

On top of all her success, Brigette published her first book right after graduating Bootcamp. She was sitting on this book for two years prior. Not only did Bootcamp connect her to Qat, the spiritual book editor, but it motivated her to finish and get it out there.

Now she serves humanity not just through her course and her mastery program, but on a whole other level. Her book allows her to reach people who might not otherwise have access to her.

She shines her light brighter than ever . . . without fear!

There are three characteristics you need to have to be able to create a 6-figure spiritual business. Watch this video to see how you score on the Success Traits Quiz. Get it here: www.areyouaspiritualentrepreneur.com.

SHIFT #5
Invest in Mentoring

5
Invest in Mentoring

"Success comes when people act together;
failure tends to happen alone."

— DEEPAK CHOPRA

OKAY, WE'RE ON to shift number five: invest in mentoring. This is a big thing because *everyone* should have a mentor. Somehow, some way.

Honestly, every successful person does. Everyone from Warren Buffett to Bill Gates to Deepak Chopra. They *all* have mentors. How do you think they got to be so successful?

It is nearly impossible to achieve success on your own. Attempting to do it all yourself is stressful, plus you just can't "see" what needs to be adjusted; you are too close to it. You need a team. You need support. You need a mentor. The names I just mentioned are as successful as they are because they invested in a mentor for themselves.

That's how you become that successful.

Mentoring brings a few things to the table: It brings clarity, it brings new ideas, and it brings accountability. Clarity, because sometimes we can't see through the weeds of what we need to do. I know, because I have a mentor, and he brings clarity to me all the time.

You remember that line at the beginning of the book, "If someone owns a doughnut shop, but also meditates, couldn't that person consider themself a spiritual entrepreneur?" That was one of the first questions my mentor asked me. I thought I had clarity on who I was serving, but clearly I hadn't thought it all the way through. Working with my mentor has been genuinely life-changing for me. A valuable mentor brings clarity. So you can see what you need to do next.

A mentor also brings new ideas. Just think about everything we've covered here. You now have all these new ideas, these new thought processes you can implement, and you have a fresh perspective on your spiritual business. Seriously, had it ever crossed your mind that earning less than six figures is selfish? Doubtful.

But now you have an understanding of why it is so important because you picked up this book and allowed me to mentor you through these six shifts.

The other thing a mentor brings is accountability, because we all know what we should be doing, but most of us aren't actually taking the steps. Does this sound familiar? I bet you have a whole list of things to do for your business, but are you actually doing them?

When we have someone whom we have to be accountable to, it's amazing what we can accomplish. This is what I'm saying here: A mentor will make sure you take action to help propel your business. You can have the most excellent ideas and the most magnificent gifts, but if you don't actually take action to do something, it doesn't work.

A great mentor will also create a community of people who are working toward similar goals, and this really multiplies everyone's effectiveness exponentially.

I have to say . . . I'm going to brag a little bit here about the community I have created; my Spiritual Biz Bootcamp and Spiritual Biz Mastery people are *amazing*. They're just an incredible group of people. The energy of these two groups of clients is off the charts, and they are there to support each other through the life-changing process of Spiritual Biz Bootcamp and Mastery. We have actually turned people away from Bootcamp because their vibration didn't match the existing group of clients; protecting the energy of the group is that important to us. Lifelong friendships are created in these groups; they call each other soul-siblings, and we even had one romance spark out of it.

Now, I'm always surprised at how many people haven't had a mentor or don't think they need one. Let me ask you this: If you don't invest in you (which really means investing in your business), or invest in a mentor to help you with your business, how can you expect your clients to invest in you? Your clients will always match your vibration. It's Universal law. Whether we like it or not, our clients *always* match our vibrations.

If you don't invest in yourself, how can you expect clients to invest in you?

If you are out there trying to find clients, but they're not coming to you, and you're struggling with that inconsistent income, you might be wondering, "Where are they, and why are they not investing in me and my amazing gifts?"

Stop and ask yourself, "If I don't invest in myself, can I really expect clients to invest in me?" Ponder that question for a moment. You honestly can't expect them to invest in you, can you? When you invest in yourself it shows the world that you are serious about your business. You are no longer an amateur being asked to do readings at birthday parties; you are a professional. It is time to make the shift. And when you make this energetic shift, it's amazing how all the energy shifts, and now you have people coming to you, and they are happy to give you the energy of money for what you do.

One of the best examples I can think of for someone who took this to the extreme is my coaching client and now friend, Qat Wanders (Her first name is pronounced "cat."). I've mentioned her in some previous chapters because she is the spiritually focused book editor who helped several of my other clients publish their books.

You know those students in school who just flourish in everything they do? The type who always graduate first in their class, the honor roll type, president of the National Honor Society, 4.2 GPA, and even graduate early? That was Qat. And Qat went through several courses before and after mine, and was always very successful. That was just kind of her thing. Even after two college degrees, she was a forever student. Always taking instruction where she could get it.

Qat found me at the beginning of 2017. And at the time, she was living in a trailer, and I don't mean the kind in a mobile home park. I mean the kind that you hitch to the back of a truck and drive around the country. She worked for a traveling circus and had for ten years! I swear, I'm not making this up.

With an English degree and a background in traditional publishing, Qat had been doing freelance book editing on the side the entire time because she could do it remotely. But because of her nomadic lifestyle, she had been previously unable to secure full custody of her daughter. She knew if she wanted her daughter full-time, she had to settle down and get her life together, so she made that her number one priority.

Qat started studying every book she could find about creating a remote business. But another obstacle was that she also dealt with severe chronic pain. This kept her from being able to work any kind of physical job or even adhere to a consistent schedule. Her nomadic lifestyle had been wearing her body down more and more by the day. She knew it wouldn't be long before she couldn't live like that any longer. So she started doing her research.

She figured out that writing and editing jobs were her best bet. It was something she could do from home. So she knew to look for people who were already doing what she wanted to do. She needed a mentor. She started this adventure in 2016, late in the year, and tried out a few different mentors. She used her savings and invested in an inexpensive program which showed her the basics of how to start a small business. It didn't bring in much income, but it was a start. She knew it was time to level up. She found another mentor who helped her take the next steps, and then another one after that.

Because she had an extensive health background as well as a yoga therapist certification, she thought her freelance writing and book editing was merely a side hustle while she worked on building her spiritual business . . . helping people overcome chronic pain on a physical, mental, and spiritual level. But she was still searching for the right mentor. Her other mentors had been very helpful in building up her side hustle while she tried to get her ducks in a row for what she really wanted to do. But none of them understood her spiritual gifts. She is a channel and an intuitive healer.

That's when she found me. She stumbled across

my webinar because those wonderful Facebook bots knew she had been clicking on every mentor out there. But when she watched mine, something clicked. She knew this was meant to be.

By the time we got on the phone, she had already made up her mind that she would work with me no matter the cost. She would figure it out. And figure it out she did. She put herself into debt for the first time in her life and dove head-first into Spiritual Biz Bootcamp.

When she first joined, she told me she wasn't sure how much time she could dedicate because her dad was sick and would likely be succumbing to cancer in the near future. We bonded over this immediately because I had already watched my mom transition to the same illness.

Well, Qat's talents were all over the place, and she didn't even know where to focus her energy. Ever heard the term herding cats? I felt like I was herding Qat! She took longer than anyone else to finish the program because things just kept coming up in her life—her relationship of six years ended, she moved in with her father and took care of him on his deathbed for three months until he passed, she moved twice, among many other things. She went through more obstacles during that time than anyone I have seen. Her life fell apart over and over, and she repeatedly picked it up and put it back together.

But she didn't give up. She took everything I said to heart and followed every step I gave her *exactly*. Even when she didn't agree, she listened to me and followed through. Her money situation wasn't looking good. She had very little and could barely eat, and was seemingly getting no closer to being able to keep her daughter. But she kept going.

An intuitive hit told me to suggest she reach out within the supportive group of other spiritual entrepreneurs and see if she could help them with some editing, proofreading, or copywriting jobs. This would give her a bit of extra money so she could sustain herself while she worked on her spiritual business.

All the other Bootcampers stepped up to the plate and hired her for all sorts of different writing and editing positions. She became the go-to gal in the group for book, blog, course, and assorted other editing help.

She made slow progress at the beginning, but all at once, everything fell into place. She started enrolling people into her Overcoming Chronic Pain Through Yoga course, which she priced at $3,000, and in the course of two weeks, brought in $18,000!

When she graduated Bootcamp, she was one of the first I invited into my Mastery program. Because she trusted me, she went ahead and signed up even though she wasn't sure how she would pay for it. While her $18,000 she made throughout Bootcamp was certainly impressive, she had still made less than $20,000 in the entire year of 2017.

But I had faith in her. And because I believed in her, she believed in herself. She trusted me as her mentor.

When she joined Mastery, it became immediately apparent that her heart wasn't in her chronic pain business as much as it was her editing business. Who would have thought? Doing all those side jobs for the other spiritual entrepreneurs, per my suggestion, had sparked something inside her.

I suggested we move her main focus to spiritual book editing and what we now call Spiritwriting, a spin-off of ghostwriting but for spiritual and channeled books. It turned out she already practiced channeled writing herself and had never bothered to mention it to me!

At this point, she had already produced two Amazon best sellers about overcoming chronic pain through yoga, so she was able to set up her course on autopilot and turn it over to someone else completely.

That allowed us to move all our attention to her spiritual writing and editing business. I knew this was the direction she needed to go, so I helped her make some shifts in the right direction. I helped her expand her business in a big way.

In 2018, she brought in just under $200,000 from her spiritual business. She increased her income tenfold! Literally. And last I checked in with her, she had brought in over $200,000 in the first five months of 2019.

She focuses on helping spiritual entrepreneurs share their divinely inspired messages with the world. She does this by writing, editing, and assisting with the publication of these books. In any phase of the process. Like I said, she is the go-to editor for everyone in my group. In fact, she is also now working with me and Spiritual Biz Publishing, the publisher for authors dedicated to shifting consciousness.

Oh, and in case you were wondering, she now has custody of her daughter. And she admits she never could have done so if she hadn't increased her financial stability so she could afford the legal fees for her costly court case.

She now lives in her own snazzy three-story house in the suburbs with her daughter, two cars, and apparently a potential guinea pig—or so her daughter says. She was able to position herself in a nice house within the best school district to look good in court. Not to mention finally being able to afford a top-notch lawyer.

Qat is a perfect example of putting your trust in a mentor with fantastic results. She never argued with me or resisted, even when she probably wanted to. She knew she was drawn to work with me for a reason, so she consciously decided to trust.

When I asked her what the biggest shift was for her that allowed her to invite abundance into her life, she said: "Finding Kimberly was like one of those soul -recognition moments for me. I knew she was the one I was looking for. I could just feel it. So I trusted my gut and, in turn, trusted her. Sure, maybe she isn't the ideal mentor for everyone out there, but she was the ideal mentor for me. That was what mattered.

"I knew if I allowed myself to trust fully, I would get the best results. She believed in me even when I didn't believe in myself, and thank God she did! Otherwise, I probably would have given up several times! But it is all worth it because my life has gone in a direction I never could have imagined. The best direction ever. And my daughter is along for the ride now."

And I think that was well said. As I mentioned

earlier, I don't just let anyone into my program. I have to know they are a good fit. And Qat was a fantastic example.

Being in vibrational alignment with your mentor is a key factor in your success. Wondering if we could be a match? Meet the Spiritual Biz Bootcamp coaches here: www.areyouaspiritualentrepreneur.com.

SHIFT #6
You Can't Help Everyone

6
You Can't Help Everyone

"Whenever you want to achieve something, keep your eyes open, concentrate
and make sure you know exactly what it is
you want. No one can hit their target with
their eyes closed."

— PAULO COELHO

ONE OF THE biggest mistakes I see spiritual entrepreneurs make is they build their business around the no-
tion that they can help everyone.

Can your gifts help everyone? In theory, yes. You have
been given something very special by Source; you are able
to heal people's hearts, minds, and souls. But, news flash,
not everyone *wants* your help. I know, crazy, isn't it?

What ends up happening when you go down the road of, "I can help everyone," is you start talking to people who don't want what you have to offer and don't want to interact with you. Have you ever tried to help a family member or good friend only to have them be completely resistant to your assistance? Or they listen to you, but they never actually take the steps necessary to get the results you can deliver?

I know I have. I have lost count of how many of my family members have asked me how to make money. As I mentioned earlier, I am half Mexican, and if you know anything at all about Latin culture, it feels like they live in a perpetual state of scarcity, and my family is no exception. "How do you do it?" they ask. I share with them my "secrets," and they do nothing with the information.

Or maybe you are hustling to get clients, but when you find a "client," they don't want to pay your prices. They want a discount, or they tell you that you are too expensive.

If you let these experiences affect you, then you will get discouraged and begin to think, "No one wants what I have . . . no one will pay for what I am offering," when the real problem is that you are trying to help the wrong people.

The key for you, as a spiritual entrepreneur, is to connect with your ideal client, the main person you are going to serve and who will get the best results. I genuinely believe that your tribe consists of the souls you have already known. These are souls you have connected with before, in a previous life, in a previous dimension, or in a different density. You have an existing connection with these souls, and they are looking for you!

The real problem is that you are trying to help the wrong people.

Now it is your job to step out as a leader and speak, so they can hear you and connect with you. These souls need to be able to recognize you.

Have you ever been to a party where it was so loud you were straining to hear the person speaking in front of you? But then suddenly you heard your name or the name of your spouse and *snap*, your ears perk up. There was a vibrational connection. That is what you need to do with your tribe. They need to be able to hear you from across a crowded room. When you talk to everyone in bulk, they disconnect from you because there is a vibrational misalignment. The souls who are looking for you are listening. They are trying to find you!

The way to attract them and interact with them is by building a soul connection with your tribe. One of the first things we do in Spiritual Biz Bootcamp is help you tap into Source to find your tribe and connect with them vibrationally. Then we spend weeks showing you how to find and connect with your tribe on a deep and intimate level so you don't even have to *think* about "selling" or "icky" marketing. Instead, you vibrationally connect with the souls you have known before. That is how you build your tribe. But you can only do this after you realize you can't serve everyone, and everyone does not want to be served by you.

I love to use this example: The Bible is the most popular book on the planet, but not everyone wants to own a Bible. So I will repeat: *not everyone wants what you offer.*

So make sure you find the right people who want to connect—those are the ones who will get the best results because they want what you have to offer, and they are committed to making a change in their lives. The mental shift you need to make is to learn to reconnect with those souls and open up space for you to get to know your tribe at an intimate level.

The final spiritual entrepreneur I would like to tell you about is Cheryl.

Cheryl is a perfect example of someone who just wanted to help everyone. And that doesn't sound like a bad thing, of course. But she was overextending herself and trying to bend over backward for people. This was leaving her worn out and drained. The fact was, her time and energy could be spent better elsewhere. But her beautiful soul struggled to accept this truth.

Aside from being a full-time French teacher, Cheryl has a program which focuses on awakening lightworkers who want to advance their skills. She starts them off with energy basics, and moves into intuitive development, and then finishes off with evidential spiritual mediumship, which she had been teaching prior to meeting me.

But at that time, she taught at a church down the road from her house. She hosted a medium development circle at a UU Fellowship for suggested donations. She passed around a basket because that was how they required her to work at that time. She had been attending circles as a medium for years, and whenever the basket came around, she would put $10–$20 in it every single time. But one day, the basket went around while she was teaching, and someone actually put pocket change in it—including pennies. I can only imagine what it felt like to look into the basket and see pennies rolling around.

Because she wasn't allowed to put a price tag on her services, she actually got nickeled and dimed. Literally! There she was, raising kids at home with her husband working, spending time away from her family after having put in a full day of work. She regularly donated two hours of her time out of the goodness of her heart to share her spiritual gift. But it was exactly that, donating.

Now you might be thinking, "That's great. She was serving, and after all, it's not all about the money." But you are wrong. It is about the money, but not for the reason you are thinking. As I mentioned earlier, when you're presenting something of value and you don't receive an energy exchange for your gifts, it shows you that the other party doesn't value what you are offering. And if they don't value it, they aren't going to be committed enough to get amazing results. See, you aren't charging for you; you are charging for *them*. When they invest in themselves, they will show up and change their lives.

This was her aha moment. And that's when she decided to schedule a discovery call with me. There were a few other factors. She was concerned because her job was iffy due to enrollment. She was never sure where it was going, so she really wanted to start teaching how to reconnect with Source and make good money doing it, but just didn't know how. And she admits she definitely had some shifts to make in terms of attitude toward money.

She started Bootcamp in August of 2017 and had eleven people enrolled into her course by November of 2017, before she even graduated Bootcamp! And they enrolled at $1,000 each. So if you're doing the math, that was $11,000.

Then her course alone made over $25,000 in 2018. Keep in mind, this is in addition to her full-time income.

She had a total of fifty enrolled at the time of this writing. That's $50,000 *extra*. And, think about it, that's also fifty lives changed. And that's on top of the 33,000 people in her How to Speak Spirit Facebook group I showed her how to start.

There were two main things she said Bootcamp helped her with: the technical knowledge of how to produce and market a full-blown online business—which she knew nothing about when she started—and then getting in alignment with it. After all, she knew she was out of alignment when she got those pennies in the basket, because even though she knew she offered a good service, it felt off balance. Learning about the energy exchange really resonated with her. It put it into a perspective she had never thought about before.

She shifted her whole mindset around money and realized it was okay to allow financial abundance into her life. Then, she began to think about how she could receive financial abundance, through her spiritual gifts, and how she would be able to share more with others and really serve.

By using her spiritual skills and helping other people, she could create a positive shift in their lives as well. That's a win-win situation.

Looking back now, there is a night-and-day difference between what her life was like before the mindset shift and what it is now. I can assure you, she no longer feels guilty about making good money.

And then there are her gifts. Growing up, there was no one else experiencing the things she was, like being able to see souls that had crossed over. Eventually, she did find a small network of people who helped her realize she wasn't crazy, but it wasn't until she joined Bootcamp and met the other incredible spiritual entrepreneurs that this was brought to a whole new level. There were so many others like her.

She spends so much time with her tribe now, and chatting with other people in the group, that she tends to forget the rest of the world doesn't even know about or believe in a lot of what she teaches. She laughs when she says she has to remind herself that not everyone feels tingles on the top of their heads ten times a day when they connect with Spirit! And now she's helping people who are right where she was years ago, those people who feel like they don't have anyone to talk to. She's helping people have a great shift in their lives and gain confidence and knowledge. What a gift indeed.

In a nutshell, she helps awakening lightworkers move forward with their spiritual gifts. Specifically, she is more geared toward spirit communication and mediumship. She has her own How to Speak Spirit program, and it's a ten-week intensive for awakening lightworkers. It begins with the very basics of how to ground and shield your energy, then how to tell your energy field from someone else's—so that's helpful for those of us who tend to take on other people's emotions.

In her program, she talks about channeling, healing energy, chakras, and auras. They also talk about working with Spirit Guides and then go into how to use all sorts of intuitive tools like pendulums or tarot cards. Next, they move into how to communicate so they can learn to hone the art of bringing in messages from loved ones from the other side and how to communicate those messages to others. She finally wraps it up with some manifestations.

What she does is absolutely fascinating! And sometimes the spirit communication all comes down to focusing on one word for evidential purposes. It's fantastic. As I talked with her, she said, just the week before, she had one of her students focus on coming up with just a single word. That student came up with Cheryl's own deceased father's password! And she says it's not a guessable word at all.

Cheryl points out that kind of bullseye evidence is impossible to compete with. Just think, when you can come up with something like that for the people you're sitting with, they know you are talking to their loved ones. You couldn't have googled it; you couldn't have guessed it. In that moment, you have done so much to remove some of the pain in the grieving process and even alleviate the fear of death. Knowing that a loved one is alive and well on the other side and that your relationship continues with them, and not only that, they are still aware of what's going on with us here in the 3D . . . just imagine how much healing that provides!

People have told Cheryl that one good session

with her did more for them than ten years in therapy. So they can create that ripple effect. How many times can I talk about that ripple effect? Hopefully it's sinking in for you by now.

Before, when she was trying to help everyone, she was giving away her time and energy at a massive level. But now, she has learned her lesson and serves these individuals at a higher level by sending them to people who can help them better, so she can keep her focus on her field of expertise.

She admits that, "You can't help everyone. It's a drain on your time and energy for sure." That was a direct quote. And I completely agree.

"Before Bootcamp, I led a mediumship development circle at a local UU fellowship at 7:30 p.m. every Monday night for pocket change. After Bootcamp, I still teach a mediumship development circle every Monday night at 7:30 p.m., online from home, to graduates of my thousand-dollar ten-week online program, How To Speak Spirit. "

A main focus of Spiritual Biz Bootcamp is to show our clients who they can serve best with their gifts. Get a sneak peek at our Avatar Manifestation Script process here: www.areyouaspiritualentrepreneur.com.

7
So What's Next?

AT THE BEGINNING of this book, I made some promises. I promised to show you how to transform your spiritual coaching business and take it from an expensive hobby to an $8,000-and-more-a-month business while serving your clients at the highest level.

Throughout this book, we talked about:

- Why earning less than six figures is being selfish. It is your duty as an awakened lightworker to step out with your gifts. This was your agreement when you came in.

- The real reason you're struggling to manifest financial abundance. We have been conditioned to believe we are not supposed to charge for our gifts. We have been told this to keep us down, worried and in a low vibration. It is time to wipe out those self-limiting beliefs and know that not only is it okay to charge for your spiritual gift, it is absolutely necessary to keep the energy flow in balance.

- The one thing that you really need to serve people around the globe. That is to create a thriving spiritual business. This is the vehicle you will use to serve this planet.

- How to create total freedom in your spiritual coaching business. *When you Make Money While You Meditate™, you can work* less while receiving more financial abundance, so you can then have that abundance to be able to give that money back out into the world.

We don't want you tied to your job. We want to make it fun. We want to make it *not* an actual job. When you're doing this, and you're doing what you love, it's not work.

You can do all this while staying 100 percent true to your spiritual calling and serving your clients at a much higher level than you are now.

For the clarity and focus required for success, here are the six shifts you need to embody to win and have a successful spiritual business.

First, you need to stop being selfish. You have a role to play here, and it is time for you to step up and share your gifts.

Second, know you should only be earning money while living your purpose. It is tainted money if it is created any other way. Make a plan to shift out of that job you cannot stand right now and live your purpose, because that's the only way you should be earning a living.

Third, use the secret weapon, which is Making Money While You Meditate™, so that your time is not tied to your income. It is time to experience the excitement of watching your bank account grow while you are meditating.

Shift number four is to see your spiritual business as a vehicle in which to serve around the globe. You really want to help people? Start serving now by turning your expensive hobby into a real business.

Shift number five: Get a mentor because you truly cannot do it on your own. You have to have guidance to really shift and to shift quickly. Having a great mentor completely speeds things up. It doesn't have to be me. There are a lot of fantastic mentors out there. Find one. Today.

Lastly, connect intimately with the souls who have known you before; they are your true tribe.

These six shifts, that we have covered here in this book, are enough to propel you to a six-figure spiritual business.

Now, I have another question for you. This is something we usually skirt over when we're thinking about things in our businesses. I want to dive into this because I think this is really important, and I know when I present this concept to people, their expression changes and they say, "I never thought about it this way."

So I want to ask you, how much is it costing you to stay where you are? This is a big thing because there is a real cost to staying exactly where you are today.

What we're going to look at first is the money side of things. I want you to look at your exact income goal. Is it $10,000 a month? Or $20,000 a month? Then I want you to examine what you earned last month. Be honest with yourself. What was that number? If you don't know how much you earned last month in your spiritual business, then take the time to figure it out. I know this isn't always fun, especially if you spent more than you brought in, but you need to know your numbers.

Next, I want you to subtract what you earned last

month from the income goal number.

Let's say your income goal is $10,000 a month; this is the amount you want to be making each month, but you only made $2,000. That's an $8,000-a-month difference. That is huge. It is costing you $8,000 a month to stay exactly where you are.

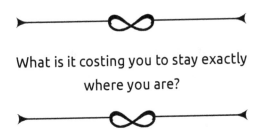

What is it costing you to stay exactly where you are?

Over a twelve-month period, that is $96,000. Over three years, that is $288,000! You cannot be blind to the potential you have inside of you and the profound impact you will have on your family's life when you take the steps to develop your business.

So, what is your number? What is it costing you to stay exactly where you are? Calculate it. Write it down. Ponder what you could be doing with your life and who you could be helping with that extra money.

Then there's the flipside of this, which is, what is it costing your soul? This is even more important than the financial cost. How long have you been working a job that doesn't feed your soul?

If you're forty-five and you've been working since you were twenty, that means that you've spent twenty-five years—that is 219,000 hours—of your life being unfulfilled if you are not yet living your purpose. That is an astronomical price to pay.

Again, what is your number? How old are you now, and how old were you when you first got trapped with golden handcuffs, making money for the sake of making money? By my calculations, I spent 183,960 hours of my life making money the "wrong" way. Now I understand why I was never satisfied with the money and why it didn't stick around. I wasn't yet living my purpose and helping people around the world.

What is your number? Not only is it costing your soul to not be living your purpose, there is also an energetic impact on your family. If you really want to help and serve your family, put your oxygen mask on first.

8
The Choice is Yours

SO NOW YOU have a choice. You can choose to take this information, this book, or maybe the notes you've been writing down, and put them on your desk and say, "I'm going to get to that later." I know what happens when that occurs. That notebook gets piled under all that unopened mail, and six months from now, you discover it. You're like, "Oh, yeah, I was going to change my life and start my spiritual business."

You can do that, or you can choose to take action *now* so that you can get out there and share your gifts with the world!

If you are inspired about changing your life so you can serve others, then Spiritual Biz Bootcamp might be the place for you. I mentioned a few times that I don't let just anyone into my program, so let's talk about the characteristics that one needs to succeed with me.

Spiritual Biz Bootcamp could be for you if . . .

- You are a spiritual teacher or coach who is *serious* about becoming a professional and creating a career with your spiritual gifts. This is not about dabbling. This is about becoming a real spiritual entrepreneur.

    Now, what does that mean? That means that you understand that being a spiritual entrepreneur and creating your business takes energy—the energy of time, the energy of money, and the energy of your creativity. Understand that those three things are absolutely necessary to create a magnificent spiritual business.

- You are creating amazing transformations with your clients. I need to know that you're doing your job and creating a ripple effect on this planet, and you're really changing your clients' lives.

- Your desire to step out with your gift to change the world is greater than your fears. I cannot stress this enough. If you have a fear of stepping out, and that fear is going to hold you back,

I truly cannot help you. You have to be ready to put that fear aside and know that you have to serve your purpose, which is stepping out and helping others.

So if you are a spiritual teacher or coach who understands that it takes the energy of time, money, and creativity to create a business and get amazing transformations for your clients, and you are ready to put your fears aside to step out in a major way, then there is a good chance you are a fit for Spiritual Biz Bootcamp.

Like I said, this is not for everyone, so let's also be clear on who this is *not* for. This is not for you if you live in a constant place of scarcity. Scarcity just brings more scarcity. When you're in that mode, that's all you're going to attract to you, so I need you to get out of scarcity mode before we can serve you. Hang in there for my *Money Is Love* book coming out in 2020, which will really help you with scarcity.

This is also not for you if you're looking to only make a few thousand dollars a month. I am dead serious when I'm talking about creating a six-figure business. If you're just looking to make an extra $1,000 or $2,000 a month, then I am not the mentor for you.

You cannot have a major effect on this planet just making $1,000 or $2,000 a month. I am looking for the person who is ready to transform their life by creating a six-figure business.

This is also not for you if you're indecisive. Being indecisive means we hem, and we haw, and we have to think about it. If we have a problem, and we ask Source for a solution, and Source delivers the answer to us, and then we have to go think about it, we've basically just told Source, "Look, I don't need you. I've got this." That's the worst place to be.

We have to be able to take inspired action, be decisive when inspiration hits. So if you're indecisive and have to think about things a lot, I'm sure it's showing up in your life in all sorts of ways, and it's going to show up in your business, too.

Also, if you're selling twenty-dollar aromatherapy oils, candles, jewelry, or any multi-level marketing, I'm not the mentor for you. But I really do wish you the best of luck in your endeavors.

If Spiritual Biz Bootcamp is calling you, then catch my free training here: www.spiritualbizsuccess.com

At the end of the training, you will have an opportunity to book a call with my team, who will make sure we are in vibrational alignment. Just imagine the impact we can have! It really is mind-blowing.

As I mentioned earlier, this is my soul contract. This is my true calling, and it is my purpose to help five thousand spiritual entrepreneurs create five thousand spiritual businesses in the next five years.

Are you one of the five thousand?

Until next time, be passionate, be inspired, and live your dream.

About the Author

 Kimberly Maska is the creator of Spiritual Biz Bootcamp, creator of *Spiritual Biz Magazine,* and CEO of Spiritual Biz Publishing. She uses her business and marketing expertise to show spiritual entrepreneurs how to Make Money While You Meditate™. She brings twenty years of business development experience to the table, including eight years on Wall Street. Marrying her business expertise with her love for consciously creating life, she shows spiritual coaches how to create financial abundance with their gifts while serving their clients at the highest level. It is her soul purpose to help five thousand spiritual entrepreneurs create five thousand businesses in the next five years.

Kimberly lives in Asheville, NC, with her husband, Daniel Pape, and their adorable pug, Bogart.

Resources

Interested in learning more about the spiritual entrepreneurs I mentioned throughout the book?

Natie and Javier

http://www.hazlodivertido.com/
http://www.josejaviercarrion.com/
http://www.nathaliejaramillo.com/

David Strickel
www.thestreamofdavid.com

Brigette Patton
www.brigettepatton.com

Qat Wanders

www.wanderingwordsmedia.com

Stacie Overman
www.stacieoverman.com

Cheryl Lynn Gramp
https://cheryl-gramp.mykajabi.com/

CPSIA information can be obtained
at www.ICGtesting.com
Printed in the USA
BVHW051650260821
615328BV00015B/782